The Easter Story

Retold by

Christopher Rawson and
The Revd. R. H. Lloyd
Chaplain of the Dragon School, Oxford

Illustrated by

Victor Ambrus

Nihil Obstat Anton Cowan *Censor*
Imprimatur David Norris, V.G.

The *Nihil obstat* and *Imprimatur* are a declaration that a book or pamphlet is considered to
be free from doctrinal or moral error. It is not implied that those who have granted the *Nihil
obstat* and *Imprimatur* agree with the contents, opinions or statements expressed.

At the beginning of Jesus' last week on Earth, he was walking to Jerusalem with his disciples. They wanted to be there for the great Jewish feast and holiday, the Passover. When Jesus reached Bethphage, near Jerusalem, he sent two disciples into the village.

"You will find a donkey and her foal tethered there," he said. "Bring them to me. If anyone asks why you are taking them, just say 'Jesus needs them'. That will be enough." He went on and was soon joined by the disciples leading the two animals.

Jesus rode into Jerusalem, through streets crowded with visitors. Many had heard exciting rumours that he was a new leader who would free them from

the Romans who had conquered their country. Shouting and cheering, they waved palm branches and spread cloaks under the donkey's hoofs.

ollowed by a large crowd, Jesus went o the Temple to pray. In the outer ourtyard, he found merchants selling attle, sheep and pigeons to visitors who ought them for their Passover acrifices. There were also money hangers sitting at their tables.

he Temple rulers allowed this to go on lthough the merchants overcharged he visitors and made huge profits.

When Jesus saw them, he was very angry. With a whip, he drove all the animals, the merchants and money changers out of the Temple. "My house should be a house of prayer," he shouted, "but you have made it a den of thieves."

The Temple rulers were furious. They knew that wherever he went, Jesus attracted crowds of followers who were spellbound by his teaching.

Caiaphas, the High Priest, called all the Jewish leaders to a meeting at his Palace. He told them that Jesus might start a rebellion against them and their Roman conquerors. They agreed that he should be put to death but they would have to arrest him secretly.

The leaders were afraid that Jesus' friends and disciples would fight to save him, and his followers would riot in the streets. Caiaphas needed an informer, a close friend of Jesus, who would tell him the best time for the arrest.

Then Judas Iscariot, one of Jesus' disciples, went to Caiaphas. "What will you give me if I betray Jesus to you?" he asked. Caiaphas gave him thirty silver coins, and from that moment Judas watched Jesus, waiting for the right time to betray him.

Jesus had made an arrangement with a friend in Jerusalem to use an upstairs room in his house for the Feast of the Passover. Jesus told Peter and John to go into the city and wait on a certain street corner until they saw a man carrying a water pot.

Peter and John went to Jerusalem and stood on the street corner. When they saw a man with a water pot, they followed him to his house.

There they told the man they were Jesus' disciples. He asked them in and showed them to a large room which they got ready for the Passover.

That night, when it was dark, Jesus and his other disciples walked into the city without being recognized. They went secretly to the house.

Judas did not know where the Feast was to be held, so he could not tell Caiaphas where Jesus would be. But he waited for his chance to give Jesus away.

In the house, Jesus and his disciples sat down for the Passover meal. It is a great Jewish Feast which celebrates the time when Moses freed the Jews from slavery in Egypt and led them across the desert to Israel.

The Jews had then been slaves in Egypt for many years and longed to return to their own land. One day, God told Moses that he would help him and his followers to escape. Moses was to tell the head of each Israelite family to kill a lamb and smear its blood on the beam above the front door of their house and on the door posts. They were then to roast the lamb and eat it with herbs and bread.

That night the Angel of God went through Egypt, killing the eldest son of every Egyptian family. No one was spared. But when the Angel came to a house with blood round the door, he passed over it. The Egyptians were so horrified, they freed the Israelites.

When Jesus had finished the Passover meal, he took a loaf of bread. He broke off a piece for each disciple and said, "Take, eat; this is my body which is given for you. Do this in remembrance of me."

Then he picked up a cup of wine. Handing it to each one in turn, he said, "Drink this all of you; for this is my blood of the new Covenant, which is shed for you and for many for the forgiveness of sins. Do this as often as you drink it in remembrance of me."

Since then, Christians have celebrated that night with a special service. It is called Holy Communion, the Holy Eucharist, the Lord's Supper, or Mass.

Then Jesus got up from his place and picked up a bowl of water and a towel. Kneeling in front of each disciple in turn, he washed and dried their feet. Usually this humble work was done only by servants for their masters.

After he had sat down again, Jesus said sadly, "Tonight one of you will betray me to my enemies." Shocked, the disciples looked at each other. Peter whispered to John, who was sitting next to Jesus, "Find out who it is!"

"Lord, who is it?" John asked Jesus. "It is the man to whom I give this piece of bread," replied Jesus, dipping it in the dish. Then he gave the bread to Judas.

"Do quickly what you have to do," he said. Judas got up from the table and left the room. He ran through the dark streets to Caiaphas' Palace.

The disciples talked angrily about Judas. But Jesus said quietly, "Tonight you will all desert me." Peter replied: "Everyone else may desert you, but I never will."

The other disciples all said the same. But Jesus turned to Peter. "I tell you, Peter," he said, "tonight, before the cock crows twice, you will deny that you know me three times."

When Judas reached the Palace, he said to Caiaphas, "I know where Jesus is.

Give me a band of Temple guards and I will lead them to him."

Jesus and his disciples left the house where they had shared the Passover meal, and walked out of Jerusalem. They crossed the river Kedron and climbed the Mount of Olives.

In the Garden of Gethsemane, Jesus led his closest disciples, Peter, James and John, away from the rest. Then he went on alone to pray to God for courage to face what lay ahead.

Judas reached the Garden of Gethsemane with the band of Temple guards. "Be careful not to arrest the wrong man in the dark," he warned them. "Jesus will be the one that I kiss."

Judas found Jesus with his disciples, waiting for him. He stepped forward and kissed Jesus on the cheek. Looking straight at him, Jesus asked quietly, "Do you betray me with a kiss?"

Brandishing their swords and clubs, the Temple guards arrested Jesus. When the disciples realized what was happening, they tried to protect Jesus from the guards.

Fighting as best they could, the disciples soon found it was hopeless. Frightened and outnumbered, they ran away in the darkness, leaving Jesus to be marched back to Jerusalem.

Jesus was taken to the High Priest's Palace to be put on trial. Although it was late at night, Caiaphas summoned as many Jewish leaders as could be found to attend the court. Caiaphas also persuaded many people to come and tell lies about Jesus.

Caiaphas began the trial, calling the witnesses. He hoped their evidence would give him the excuse to condemn Jesus to death. But when Caiaphas asked them questions, everyone could see that they were making up the answers and the evidence was not true.

When Caiaphas realized that his plan to convict Jesus would not work, he turned to Jesus and said, "You have heard what the witnesses have said about you. What have you got to say?"

Jesus, who had been silent all through the trial, just looked at Caiaphas and still did not answer him.

At last, Caiaphas lost his patience, and said to Jesus, "I will ask you one more question and you must give me an answer. "Are you the Son of God?"

The court waited in silence until Jesus replied, "It is you who says it." Then Caiaphas turned to the crowd and asked for their verdict. "He is guilty," they shouted. "He must die."

While the trial was taking place at the High Priest's Palace, Peter made his way back into Jerusalem. Walking quietly through the dark streets, he slipped into the Palace courtyard.

He was determined to find out what was happening to Jesus and stood with a group of men who were warming themselves round an open fire.

As he listened to them talking, a servant girl passed him. Looking hard at him, she said, "Surely you were one of the followers of the man they call Jesus of Nazareth?"

But Peter denied it, saying, "I do not understand what you mean. I don't know anyone called Jesus." As he spoke, a cock crowed in the darkness.

A few minutes later, another servant walked past. She stopped when she saw Peter and said to the men, "This fellow was with Jesus of Nazareth." Again Peter denied it, saying loudly, "I do not know the man".

Shortly afterwards, a man came up to Peter and stared at him. "Surely you are another of them," he said. "Your accent gives you away." Peter was frightened and shouted angrily, "I tell you, I do not know the man."

As he spoke, the cock crowed again. Hearing it, Peter turned round and saw Jesus looking at him. Then he remembered that Jesus had said to him, "Before the cock crows twice, you will deny that you know me three times."

He ran from the courtyard and hid in the darkness outside, knowing he had behaved like a coward. When Judas heard that Jesus had been condemned to death, he was horrified at what he had done, and killed himself.

After sentencing Jesus to death, Caiaphas and the other Jewish leaders took him to Pontius Pilate, the Roman governor of Jerusalem, for trial.

They knew that although they had found Jesus guilty, they were not allowed to put him to death. He had to be tried and sentenced by a Roman court because only a Roman court had the power to carry out an execution.

It was not an offence under Roman law, to claim to be the Son of God, so Caiaphas told Pilate that Jesus claimed to be the King of the Jews. This meant he was setting himself up as a leader against the Romans, which was a crime punishable by death.

Pilate asked Jesus what he had to say to the charge. To Pilate's surprise, Jesus did not answer him.

After hearing the evidence, Pontius Pilate realized that Jesus was innocent. But he did not want to anger the Jewish leaders by saying so.

Every year, at the time of Passover, it was the custom for the Roman governor to release one prisoner from jail. Pilate thought that if the crowd asked for Jesus to be freed, it would solve the problem of what to do with him. So he asked the crowd, "Shall I release Jesus or Barabbas?"

"Barabbas, Barabbas," shouted the crowd. Pilate was surprised because Barabbas was a dangerous criminal. But the Chief Priests and leaders had persuaded the crowd to ask for Barabbas to be freed.

"What shall I do with Jesus?" Pilate then asked the crowd. "Crucify him!" they shouted. "What harm has he done?" asked Pilate. But the crowd just shouted even louder, again and again, "Crucify him! Crucify him!"

17

To satisfy the crowd, Pilate gave the order for Jesus to be crucified, even though he knew he was innocent. Soldiers took Jesus away and whipped him while Pilate washed his hands to show that he did not accept the blame.

The soldiers dressed Jesus in a scarlet robe, pressed a crown of thorns down on his head and put a stick in his hand. Laughing and jeering at him, they called him "King of the Jews". They spat in his face and whipped him again.

When they were tired of mocking him, the soldiers dressed Jesus in his own clothes again. They made him carry the beam of a cross through the streets of Jerusalem to the place where those condemned to death were crucified.

Jesus was very tired and weak from the whipping. Again and again he fell down because the beam was so heavy. A Roman soldier ordered a man watching the procession to carry the beam. His name was Simon of Cyrene.

18

The place where Jesus was crucified was called Golgotha, which means "Place of the Skull". The soldiers nailed Jesus to the cross. At the same time they crucified two robbers, one each side of him. Pontius Pilate ordered a notice to be fixed to the cross above Jesus' head. On it were the words "Jesus of Nazareth, King of the Jews".

When the Jewish leaders read the notice which had been fixed to Jesus' cross, they were very angry. Some of them hurried off to Pontius Pilate to complain.

"You should have written 'Jesus of Nazareth, who claimed to be King of the Jews'," they said. But Pilate sent them away, saying, "What I have written, I have written."

After the Roman soldiers had nailed Jesus to the cross, they divided his clothes amongst themselves. Each took one garment.

His tunic was woven in one piece and had no seams. The soldiers said, "We must not tear this. It's too valuable." So they threw dice for it.

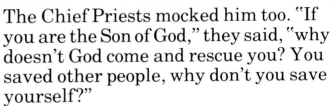

While Jesus was hanging on the cross, some of his enemies arrived. Looking up at him, they said, "If you really are the Son of God, come down from the cross and we will believe you."

The Chief Priests mocked him too. "If you are the Son of God," they said, "why doesn't God come and rescue you? You saved other people, why don't you save yourself?"

Mary, Jesus' mother, was standing near the cross with John, one of Jesus' disciples. When Jesus looked down, he saw them there and asked John to take care of his mother like a good son.

At mid-day, the sky grew dark. Jesus cried out in great pain, "I am thirsty." A soldier soaked a sponge in sour wine, fixed it to the end of his spear and held it up to Jesus' lips.

Slowly the hours passed while the small crowd near Jesus' cross watched and waited. At three o'clock, Jesus lifted his head and spoke the prayer every Jew said before going to sleep, "Father, into thy hands I commit my spirit."

Then Jesus bowed his head and died. A Roman soldier who was standing near the cross looked up at Jesus and said, "Truly this man was a son of God." Silent with sorrow, the crowd drifted back to the city.

22

A wealthy man, called Joseph of Arimathea, went to Pontius Pilate and asked him for permission to remove Jesus' body. "I have a tomb ready and would like to give this man a proper burial," he said. Pilate ordered that Jesus' body should be given to him.

Joseph and some other friends of Jesus took his body down from the cross and wrapped it in a clean linen sheet. They carried it to the tomb which Joseph owned, which had been cut out of solid rock on a hill outside the walls of Jerusalem.

When they reached the tomb, they carried the body inside. There they began the preparations for burial. But as it was now Friday evening and the beginning of the Jewish Sabbath, they did not have time to finish.

The Jewish Sabbath is on Saturday. It begins at sunset on Friday evening and Jews are not supposed to work after that time. So Jesus' friends had to leave their final preparations for the burial until Sunday morning.

When they left the tomb, Joseph and Nicodemus rolled a huge round slab of stone across the entrance.

Mary of Magdala and Mary, the mother of Joseph, were there and saw where Jesus' body had been laid.

In Jerusalem, the Chief Priests and other Jewish leaders went to Pontius Pilate to ask for his help. "Do you remember that Jesus prophesied he would be raised from the dead after three days?" they said.

"Will you give orders for soldiers to stand guard over the tomb? Otherwise his friends may go and secretly take the body away. Then they will tell everyone that Jesus' body is not in the tomb because he has come alive again."

Pontius Pilate agreed to this request. He commanded that four of his soldiers should guard the tomb night and day, watching the entrance all the time.

Early on Sunday morning, Mary of Magdala and two friends went to the tomb, carrying perfumed oils and spices to finish the burial preparations.

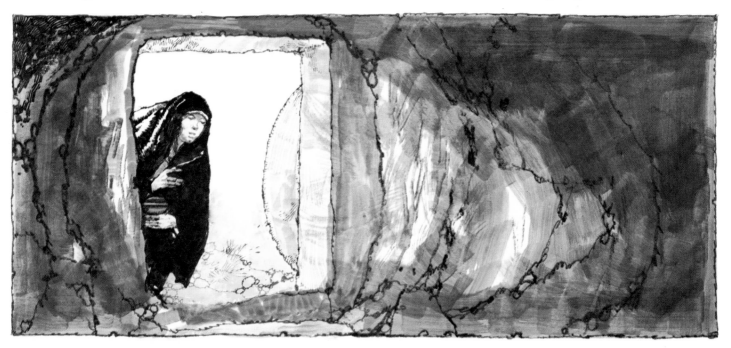

They wondered if any of the men would come to move the heavy stone for them. But when they reached the tomb, they were astonished to see that the stone had already been rolled away from the entrance.

The soldiers who should have been guarding the tomb were not there. Suddenly afraid, Mary of Magdala looked into the tomb. She was filled with dismay when she saw that the body of Jesus had gone.

Mary and her friends ran back to Jerusalem to tell the disciples what had happened. On the way, they met Peter and John. "They have taken the Lord from the tomb," wept Mary, "and we do not know where they have laid him."

When Peter and John heard this, they ran as fast as they could to the tomb. John, who was younger than Peter and could run faster, arrived first. But he did not want to go in on his own. He waited outside for Peter.

Together they went into the tomb and saw that Jesus' body was no longer there. But they could not understand what had happened.

The linen sheet which had been wrapped around the body was still lying on the ledge. The cloth which had covered his head was there too.

Later that day, Mary of Magdala went back to the tomb. She was heartbroken at the thought that someone had stolen Jesus' body and hidden it. She knelt near the entrance, quietly weeping.

While she was there, Jesus came and stood beside her. "Why are you weeping? Who are you looking for?" he asked her. Mary did not look up. She thought it must be the gardener.

She answered, "If it is you, sir, who have removed him, tell me where you have laid him, and I will take him away."

Jesus said, "Mary!" Then she looked at him and recognizing who he was, she cried out with joy, "My Master!"

Later the same day, two of Jesus' friends were walking along the road to Emmaus, which was about seven miles west of Jerusalem. As they walked, they sadly talked about everything that had happened at the weekend.

A third man joined them and they told him how disappointed they were. "We really believed that Jesus was the Messiah," they said. "But he couldn't have been. No Messiah would have allowed himself to be crucified."

The third man disagreed with them. Quoting from the scriptures, he explained that it had been prophesied that the Messiah would have to die. The discussion was so interesting that when they reached Emmaus, they invited him to stay the night.

After sitting down at the table for supper, the stranger picked up a loaf of bread, and when he had blessed it, he divided it and offered each of them a piece. At that moment, they realised who he was. "Jesus!" they said in astonishment.

The two disciples went back to Jerusalem to tell the others. At first, no one believed them. Later, ten of Jesus' disciples met in the upstairs room. Thomas was not there, nor was Judas Iscariot, who was dead.

Then Jesus appeared among them and said, "Peace be with you." At first they were frightened, thinking they were looking at a ghost. They were only convinced it really was him when they saw the nail marks in his hands.

Later the disciples met Thomas who had not been there when Jesus appeared. They told him what had happened, but he would not believe them. He said, "I will not believe it is really Jesus unless I can feel the nail marks in his hands."

The following Sunday they were all together in the upstairs room. Jesus appeared again and told Thomas to feel his wounds. When Thomas had done this, he could not doubt any longer that it really was Jesus. He whispered, "My Lord and my God!"

Jesus appeared several times to his followers during the forty days after his death. He wanted them to be sure he had risen from the dead and to teach them what they must do.

Then he visited them one last time and walked with them from Jerusalem to the Mount of Olives. There he gave them his last instructions.

"You must go back to Jerusalem and wait until the Holy Spirit comes on you," he said. "Then go out and spread my message everywhere. Remember, I shall always be with you."

When he had said this, he moved away from them until he was hidden by a cloud and they could see him no longer.

The eleven disciples returned to Jerusalem and waited for the Holy Spirit to come, praying constantly.

During the next few days, Peter made a suggestion. "Jesus chose twelve of us to be his disciples, but now Judas is dead we are only eleven. We must choose someone who knew and loved Jesus to take Judas' place."

The other disciples agreed and about a hundred and twenty followers of Jesus met to elect a new disciple. Two men, Joseph and Matthias, were put forward.

After praying to God to help them choose the right one, they all voted. And it was Matthias who was elected to be the twelfth disciple.

Ten days after they last saw Jesus, the Jewish Feast of Pentecost was celebrated in Jerusalem, and the city was crowded with pilgrims from many lands. This Feast reminds Jews of the time when God gave Moses the Ten Commandments on Mount Sinai.

The disciples were all together, waiting and praying for the Holy Spirit. Suddenly the room was filled with a noise like a roaring wind, and flames like fire appeared and settled on the head of each one of them. Immediately they were all filled with the power of the Holy Spirit.

A complete change came over each one of the disciples. They rushed into the crowded streets of Jerusalem and told everyone they met about Jesus.

The new faith of Christianity spread through the city and out across the country and, later, the world. For almost two thousand years since then, Christianity has survived and grown in strength. Now one third of all people in the world are Christians – that is, one thousand million people.